Dog Tales:
True Stories About Amazing Dogs

Helping Dogs

Dog Tales:
True Stories About Amazing Dogs

Distinguished Dogs
Helping Dogs
Hunting and Herding Dogs
Police Dogs
Search and Rescue Dogs

Dog Tales:
True Stories About Amazing Dogs

Helping Dogs

Marie-Therese Miller

CHELSEA
CLUBHOUSE
An Imprint of Chelsea House Publishers

Helping Dogs
© 2007 by Infobase Publishing

Chelsea Clubhouse
An imprint of Infobase Publishing
132 West 31st Street
New York, NY 10001

ISBN-10: 0-7910-9035-3
ISBN-13: 978-0-7910-9035-0

Library of Congress Cataloging-in-Publication Data
Miller, Marie-Therese.
   Helping dogs / Marie-Therese Miller.
      p. cm.—(Dog tales, true stories about amazing dogs)
   Includes bibliographical references and index.
   ISBN 0-7910-9035-3 (hardcover)
   1. Guide dogs—Juvenile literature.   I. Title.
   HV1780.M55 2007

362.4'183—dc22

Chelsea House and Chelsea Clubhouse books are available at special discounts when purchased in bulk quantities for businesses, associations, institutions, or sales promotions. Please call our Special Sales Department in New York at (212) 967-8800 or (800) 322-8755.

You can find Chelsea House and Chelsea Clubhouse on the World Wide Web at http://www.chelseahouse.com

Development Editor: Anna Prokos
Text Design: Annie O'Donnell
Cover Design: Ben Peterson

Printed in the United States of America

Bang FOF 10 9 8 7 6 5 4 3 2 1

This book is printed on acid-free paper.

All links and Web addresses were checked and verified to be correct at the time of publication. Because of the dynamic nature of the Web, some addresses and links may have changed since publication and may no longer be valid.

Contents

1

Guide Dog Puppyhood

Rigby is a Labrador retriever puppy with silky black fur and large, curious eyes. While this dog may look like a regular pup, Rigby is no ordinary pet. This special canine is training to be a guide dog. One day, his big eyes may act as the eyes for a blind person. That's because Rigby is a puppy-in-training for Guiding Eyes for the Blind, an organization that breeds, trains, and places guide dogs with people who need them. The group makes sure Rigby, and other dogs like him, are taught the proper skills they need to be of service to their future handlers.

BRINGING UP PUP

Rigby was born at the Guiding Eyes for the Blind Canine Development Center in Patterson, New York. The dog is only one of 600 puppies born at the center each year. The Guiding Eyes organization breeds its own dogs and trains its healthiest and smartest pups for guide dog work. A guide dog must be intelligent, willing to work, and have a calm disposition.

BREEDING SUCCESSFUL GUIDE DOGS

What makes a guide dog successful? Experts say a good guide dog starts with proper breeding. Guiding Eyes for the Blind breeds its own dogs at its Breeding and Placement Center in Patterson, New York. The staff strives to breed the healthiest dogs with personality characteristics best suited for their future jobs as guide dogs.

The breeding staff chooses a pair of dogs for the best breeding success. The mother dogs, called broods, and father dogs, known as studs, are chosen to breed because of their high scores on guide dog tests. These dogs are the most intelligent canines and are also the most resilient and calm of all the dogs evaluated. Their willingness to work makes them top picks for breeding. The staff hopes the puppies will share their parents' **temperament**.

For this reason, Labrador retrievers, like Rigby, make good guide dogs. In addition, Guiding Eyes includes golden retrievers and German shepherds in their guide dog training program. Like Labrador retrievers, these dogs are hard-working canines that are willing to help people.

From the moment Rigby and his sibling pups were born, staff members at the center kept an eye on the group to make sure they stayed healthy and safe. Rigby and his dog family lived in a large kennel that was kept extremely clean and germ-free. Keeping germs away from these valuable newborn puppies

Before breeding choices are made, the staff checks the physical health of the broods and studs. Labrador retrievers suffer from hip dysplasia, a problem with the hip joint that can cripple a dog. A guide dog couldn't continue its work if it suffered from this serious disorder. Because of the strict breeding criteria at Guiding Eyes, only six percent of their dogs have this condition.

Recently, Guiding Eyes breeding specialists have experimented with combining dog breeds. They want to see if top quality mixed-breed dogs can perform even better as guide dogs. So far, the center has bred Labrador retrievers with golden retrievers. This mixed breed, which the center calls GLABS, takes the best qualities of both types of dogs and combines them into one. Will this mixed breed perform as well as Guiding Eyes' other dogs? Only time can tell, but Guiding Eyes staff is hopeful that GLABS will make top-notch guide dogs.

is important. People who enter the kennel area step into a shallow pan of bleach solution so that illnesses won't be caused by whatever is on people's shoes. Before handling any of the pups, staff members and Center volunteers wash their hands with surgical soap, the strong cleansing soap doctors use in a hospital setting. These steps ensure that the pups stay healthy.

When Rigby was just one week old, volunteers visited the puppy. These volunteers are called early **socializers** because they introduce guide dog puppies to social situations. The socializers massage the puppies from ears to paws. The puppies have to adjust to frequent human touch because their guide dog users will handle them often to groom them and check for illnesses. The volunteers also take the puppies to a playroom filled with toys, where the dogs trot across tile floors, rug squares, and textured rubber mats. Guide dog puppies must accept the feel of different material under their paws.

The puppies balance on tipping saucers, climb through tunnels, and chase balls. The dogs have fun, but they also learn to be confident with new experiences, a necessary skill for a guide dog.

When Rigby was between six and eight weeks of age, home socializer volunteers took the pup to their house for three to five days at a time. This was Rigby's first chance to leave the Center and separate from his dog family to become part of a human family.

PUPPY TESTING

During Rigby's first nine weeks of life, he was tested three times to see if he would make a successful guide dog. The puppy evaluators bring

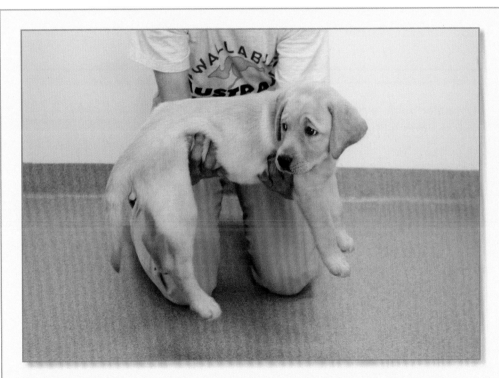

Evaluators lift a puppy off the ground, which makes the dog's feet dangle for a minute. This tests if the dog can remain calm.

A handler holds a puppy with its back against the floor in order to test how the dog will accept an unusual positions.

each puppy into a room and put it through a series of tasks.

At first, the puppy is lifted off the ground, its legs dangling for a minute before the dog is placed down. Then, it is gently held with its back against the floor. The evaluators look for a puppy that is calm and quick to forgive its handler for placing it in an unusual position.

During another part of the test, an evaluator opens an umbrella with a loud pop. Next, she shakes and

Startle tactics, such as opening an umbrella and shaking a loud cookie tin, test how a puppy reacts to noise.

drops a noisy cookie tin. These startle tactics let an evaluator know if the puppy will run from the noisy objects or approach them with curiosity and confidence. Puppies that don't react well to noise won't make good guide dogs. Guide dogs must stay calm in noisy situations. They cannot shiver or hide, for example, when they hear a car engine roar. They must stay calm and close to their blind handlers at all times.

Guide dogs should also be energetic and curious enough to investigate new situations. To test this, an evaluator tosses a ball of paper for the puppy to fetch and rolls a toy duck across the floor. If the puppy bounds after the paper ball or follows the waddling duck, the puppy has proved itself to be energetic and curious.

After the first two tests, the home socializers are given a puppy report card, which outlines the pup's weak areas. The socializers work to help the puppy improve its lower scores. If the puppy didn't perform well during its handling test, for example, the socializer will try to hold the puppy more.

Puppies must fully pass the third test. Otherwise, they are released from the guide dog program and put on another path. A released puppy might be sent for training as a police detector dog or as an assistance dog to help someone who uses a wheelchair.

Some puppies are placed in homes where they will be cherished as a family pet. Rigby passed his third test with flying colors; he was on his way to becoming a guide dog.

Raising Rigby

An article in a local newspaper quickly caught the attention of 11-year-old Nicole Ravetto and her 13-year-old brother Mark. The siblings saw that Guiding Eyes for the Blind was seeking volunteers to raise puppies and prepare them for formal guide dog training. Nicole and Mark jumped at the chance to become puppy raisers.

"We wanted to do something for a good cause," says Nicole. After discussing the idea with their mother, the children decided to volunteer.

The Ravettos worked hard at training Rigby and are proud of the pup's accomplishments during training and testing.

The puppy raisers-in-training attended four classes, which taught them about the responsibilities of raising a puppy. Nicole and Mark also puppy-sat for a few pups, which allowed them some hands-on experience with what it takes to care for young dogs.

As Nicole and Mark finished their training to become puppy raisers, Rigby passed his puppy evaluation and was ready to be given to a family. The professional staff at Guiding Eyes for the Blind makes sure that a puppy's personality and a potential raiser's lifestyle are a good mix. An overly active puppy, for example, might be sent to a busy home with five energetic children who are constantly on the move. On the flip side, a calm pup might be raised and trained in a household with fewer children. The Guiding Eyes staff considered Rigby's personality and the Ravetto's lifestyle and decided that the two would make an excellent match.

Once Rigby moved in with the Ravettos, Nicole and Mark made sure the pup felt comfortable in his new surroundings. They showed Rigby around the house so he could become used to the sounds of a house. If Rigby became startled with the sounds of the doorbell or the dishwasher, the children reassured the pup. Soon, Rigby became familiar with the home environment, and the dog training began.

Nicole and Mark's job was to teach Rigby basic obedience, like how to sit, stay, and walk on a leash.

They had to expose the dog to many different experiences to help the future guide dog be at ease in any situation.

Rigby learned how to climb up the stairs in the Ravetto's home with Nicole's patient teaching. She stood at the top and encouraged him. When he reached her, she patted him and said, "Good dog, Rigby." With every successful climb, Rigby received a lot of praise and petting. Puppy raisers for Guiding Eyes don't give the pups treats or people food for good behavior because the dogs need to stay trim and healthy. Plus, guide dogs have to learn to eat their own food at the proper times.

The family also had to housebreak Rigby, to teach him to go to the bathroom outside. During their housebreaking strolls, they taught Rigby to "get busy." This command lets the dog know when it's time to go to the bathroom. In time, Rigby would learn to go on command. This way, a blind handler won't have a guide dog that stops walking to take a bathroom break.

The Ravettos also taught Rigby the proper way to walk on a leash. Guide dogs don't heel, that is, walk right next to their handlers. Guide dogs must take the lead, so they are taught to walk to the left of the handler and a few steps ahead.

When Rigby was six months old, the pup earned his "Guiding Eyes Puppy in Pre-training" vest. This

Puppies that wear the Guiding Eyes Puppy in Pre-training vest are usually allowed to go to places where guide dogs are permitted. The vest lets others know the dog is working.

allowed Nicole and Mark to take Rigby to many places where guide dogs—but not pet dogs—were permitted. Guide dogs are allowed to accompany their handlers to any public place. Nicole and Mark took the pup to the mall and to fast-food restaurants. When Rigby was used to various situations, he went on to his next big adventure.

To expand the dog's experience, Guiding Eyes "switches out" puppies in training. Every so often, the dog spends time with another puppy raiser in a completely different environment. For example, a pup being raised in the city, with the noises of traffic and crowds, might go to stay with a farm family, where it will be surrounded by horses and tractors. Rigby was switched out to a prison, where he spent one month being cared for by an inmate who volunteered for a program called Puppies Behind Bars.

IN FOR TRAINING

After more than a year of being trained, cared for, and loved by the Ravettos, Rigby's big day had arrived. It was time for the dog to take a test to see if he was ready to start formal guide dog training. This evaluation is known as "in for training."

Rigby and the other pups were escorted to an outdoor testing course. The puppy raisers were led to a conference room, where they could watch the test

PUPPIES BEHIND BARS

Puppies Behind Bars is an organization that works with prison inmates to raise Guiding Eyes for the Blind puppies. The program has mentally healthy inmates who've had at least one year of good behavior in prison raise puppies that may one day become guide dogs.

Participants in the Puppies Behind Bars program learn how to train and care for their dogs and can feel a sense of accomplishment in the dogs' success.

Puppies who partici-pate in the Puppies Behind Bars program have a great advantage: They have 'round-the-clock human attention. From the time the pup and inmate wake, the two spend the day together. The puppy accompanies the inmate to work, which might be, for example, in the prison library or laundry. In the afternoon, it's the puppy's turn to work as the inmate practices obedience commands with the dog. Each day ends with the inmate grooming the puppy and giving the pup a full-body massage.

Because a prison is like a self-contained town, the puppies have experiences similar to puppies training outside the prison gates. However, there are some things the puppies don't encoun-ter in prison, such as cars and supermarkets. To experience these situations, volunteers take the puppies home for two weekends a month and one day each week. During these visits, the pup-pies also have a chance to encounter household sights and sounds. Some puppies can even head into a big city for "urban

(continues)

(continued)

socialization," where they become accustomed to the bustle of crowds and boarding subways and buses.

The inmates benefit from the Puppies Behind Bars program, too. The program gives them the opportunity to be responsible for an animal's life and to contribute to society in a positive way. By raising a puppy, the inmates build skills that can be used in the work force when they are released from prison.

through a large window. Nicole and Mark hoped that their hard work would help Rigby succeed.

At first, the trainer had Rigby respond to basic commands. Then, she walked Rigby across a textured mat to test his skills on different materials. In the course of day, a guide dog might step upon ice, tile or carpeted floors, or metal grates. The dog must continue to work with various textures under its paws.

Next, Rigby was tested for his reaction to noise. The trainer had him sit, and then a person shot a starter pistol from about 50 feet (15.24 meters) away. The evaluators do not want to see a dog that attempts to bolt or one that cowers in fear. Guide dogs need to work even when loud noises are present.

THE FIRST GUIDE DOG IN THE UNITED STATES

In the 1920s, American Dorothy Harrison Eustis bred and trained German shepherds in Switzerland. Her dogs were used to help the Swiss Army and European police departments. During her time in Switzerland, Eustis visited a school in Germany where she watched dogs being trained to guide wounded soldiers who had been blinded during World War I.

Eustis wrote an article about these guide dogs for *The Saturday Evening Post*, a popular magazine at that time. The story, called "The Seeing Eye," was published on November 5, 1927—and it received lots of attention.

Many visually impaired Americans wrote letters to Eustis asking her to train guide dogs for them. Morris Frank, a 16-year-old from Tennessee who had been blind since childhood, sent a letter to the dog trainer. He made Eustis a serious offer. If Eustis could pair him with a guide dog, he would travel across the United States to show how guide dogs help disabled people regain their independence.

Shortly after receiving his letter, Eustis had Frank come to Switzerland and work with a guide dog, a female German shepherd named Buddy. As promised, Frank traveled the country with Buddy to show what a guide dog team could accomplish. During their journeys, Frank and Buddy challenged the "No Dogs Allowed" signs that were often found in public places.

In February 1929, Eustis and Frank started The Seeing Eye guide dog school in Nashville, Tennessee. Today, based out of New Jersey, The Seeing Eye, Inc., breeds and trains German shepherds, Labrador retrievers, and golden retrievers for work as guide dogs. Thanks to Buddy, thousands of people have turned to guide dogs for increased independence.

The trainer then walked Rigby toward a man with an umbrella, who popped it open. The trainer and Rigby circled around and passed the man a second time. Again, he opened the umbrella with a snap. The dog should not try to hide behind his handler when the umbrella surprises him. At the end of the test, the man held the closed umbrella by his side and approached Rigby. The evaluators are seeking a dog that will not seem worried by the man, and one that might even approached him curiously. Guide dogs need to face different challenges with confidence.

After Rigby was tested, the Ravettos received the good news. Their pup passed the "in for training" evaluation. The time had come for Nicole and Mark to bid farewell to Rigby. They were sad to see him go, but they were proud of Rigby's accomplishments. The growing pup had an important job ahead.

First Steps in Training

Guiding Eyes dogs that pass the in-for-training evaluation move on to the Guiding Eyes for the Blind Headquarters and Training Center in Yorktown Heights, New York. The dogs stay in large indoor kennels with one or two kennel mates. The dogs face their toughest training yet: formal guide dog training.

The Guiding Eyes trainers are well-prepared to teach the dogs what they need to know to become working guides. Each trainer is assigned a group of about ten dogs that will train together for up to four months.

During the first phase of training, trainers and their dogs work on the quiet suburban streets surrounding the Center. The trainers reinforce the basic obedience commands that the dogs learned with their puppy raisers. The verbal commands are accompanied with hand gestures. For example, the "down" vocal command is paired with the hand held palm down, while the "up" command has the hand held palm up.

At this point in training, the dogs become accustomed to wearing a working harness. The harness consists of leather straps that fit behind a dog's front legs and across its upper chest. Attached to the straps, at the dog's back, is a stiff U-shaped handle, which the guide dog user will grip. In addition, the dogs wear a leash.

The most important lesson the dogs learn at this time is how to respond to the command "forward." On "forward," the dogs learn to walk a bit ahead of the trainer at a consistent speed and with a constant pull on the harness. The dogs are also trained to walk in a straight line, which will make it easier for the blind handler to keep track of her location,

One of the challenges of training guide dogs is to keep the dogs from being distracted by wildlife. Labrador and golden retrievers were originally bred as hunting dogs, so these breeds have a strong instinct

Guide dogs walk to the left and a few steps ahead of their blind handler in order to lead the way.

to chase prey, such as squirrels or birds. The trainers work hard to change this behavior, and they make sure to praise the pup for the progress it makes.

PHASE TWO

With each new phase of training, the dogs are exposed to busier, more challenging environments. For the second phase of Guiding Eyes' training, the trainers and dogs work in the medium-sized town of Peekskill, New York.

Here, the dogs learn to respond to the directional commands "right" and "left." In addition, the trainers teach the dogs to stop at changes in elevation, such as curbs or ramps. This will allow the guide

TRAINING DOGS FOR SPECIAL NEEDS

Guiding Eyes for the Blind trains dogs to provide mobility for blind individuals who have additional special needs. The Guiding Eyes personnel visit the home of the special needs applicant to observe the person closely. This observation allows Guiding Eyes staff to decide what type of dog would best meet the person's special requirements. For example, an individual with balance problems might need a large, strong dog that can be used for support. A person who has arthritis in her hands might need a patient dog because it may take longer to put the dog in the harness.

Special needs canines undergo eight months to one year of training, as compared to three to four months of training that dog user to tap her foot and find the curb. Then she can step up or down safely.

During the second phase of training, the dogs are trained to pick up the pace when crossing a street. The dog and his blind handler must cross quickly and safely before the light turns or cars approach.

The second training phase also teaches the dogs to indicate the location of doorknobs and elevator buttons by walking directly up to the objects. To teach this skill, the trainers place dog treats close to the door handles or elevator buttons, which entices the dogs to move toward the desired item.

When the dogs master the first two phases of training, they are ready to tackle the more advanced

a regular guide dog requires. The special needs of the handler will determine the type of additional training the dog will receive. If the guide dog user is deaf and blind, for example, the canine might be trained to respond to hand commands instead of verbal ones. A dog that's being trained for this applicant will be rewarded with physical praise, such as patting, rather than spoken praise. A person with a cane, for instance, might not be able to use hand gestures to direct the dog, so the dog will be trained to respond only to verbal commands. These are just some examples of how guide dogs obtain special needs training to help their handlers.

After months of formal training, a special needs guide dog will be paired with its new user. Both dog and user will attend a 26-day class at Guiding Eyes to learn to work together as a team.

Guide dogs in training are exposed to street scenes in which they learn to stop at curbs or ramps.

training. Phases three and four take place in bustling cities, and the tasks required of the dogs are more complex. These challenging environments help the dogs build skills and adapt to changing situations.

Advanced Guide Dog Training

In the first two phases of formal guide dog training, the dogs learn to move straight forward with a consistent speed and pull, stop at changes in elevation, and to respond to directional commands. Phases three and four use these lessons to teach the dogs more complicated skills. At various times in the last stages of training, a blindfolded instructor works with each dog to gauge how it will perform with a person who can't see.

The third phase of Guiding Eyes training occurs in the small city of White Plains, New York. During this time, the dogs learn to avoid obstacles in a path, such as street signs or parking meters. In addition, the trainers teach each dog to bypass objects overhead, such as tree branches. Not only does the dog have to walk around these dangers, it must also make sure its handler doesn't bump into anything.

To teach this skill, the trainers gesture away from the obstacle and guide the dog in the desired direction using the leash. If the dog does not allow enough room for the trainer to avoid the hazard, the trainer slaps the item loudly. The dog hears the loud noise and feels a jerk on the harness. These signals show

CHOOSING A DIFFERENT PATH

Not every dog that enters formal training becomes a guide dog. Some dogs may show signs of stress, making it necessary for the dog to leave the program.

The experts at Guiding Eyes for the Blind say that dogs that aren't suited for guide dog work have the opportunity to go into other programs. Many of these dogs enter training for the Bureau of Alcohol, Tobacco, Firearms, and Explosives. These dogs learn to be narcotics or explosive detection dogs. They find illegal drugs or bombs by using their keen sense of smell.

An explosive detection dog needs to be intelligent and willing to work, just as a guide dog does. However, a bomb detection dog can rely completely on the commands of its handler. The

the dog that it has made a mistake. Then, the trainer and dog will try again.

During this training phase, a Guiding Eyes dog is also taught how to disobey a command in order to protect its handler. This is known as **intelligent disobedience.** This type of training gets the dog accustomed to tricky situations, such as stopping at the edge of a train platform. To teach this skill, the trainers and their dogs go to the local train station. The dogs are taught that even if their handlers command "forward," they must turn to the right and lead the handlers away from the edge. This training helps build a dog's confidence in order to ignore a direct command.

dog does not have to use the intelligent disobedience a guide dog uses. This can be less demanding for the dog.

Narcotics and explosive detection dogs are encouraged to use their natural scenting instincts in their work. On the other hand, guide dogs must learn to curb some of their instincts, such as chasing prey, in order to perform well. Working against instincts can be stressful for a dog, so a guide dog in training that shows signs of stress could be shifted to this type of detective work.

Some released guide dogs go on to work as therapy dogs, while others become treasured family pets. Whatever the dog's final career, its breeding and training at Guiding Eyes for the Blind will help the dog succeed in life.

An important part of a guide dog's job is to protect its handler from moving cars. That's where lessons called traffic training come into play. The first portion of traffic training takes place on less-traveled roads. At first, a Guiding Eyes expert drives a car from a driveway onto the sidewalk where the trainer and the dog are walking. The trainer teaches the dog to stop when a moving car comes close. If the car is dangerously near, the dog learns to walk backward in a straight line to avoid the hazard.

Next, the dog is exposed to a variety of traffic situations. The training car might turn toward the dog from the right or left. It could back up from a driveway with the dog close by. The trainer tries to give the dog plenty of practice before it faces true-life traffic.

ON THE ROAD

The last phase of traffic training takes place in actual traffic conditions. The trainers and dogs work together to cross busy intersections. At each intersection, a guide dog user is responsible for listening to the sound of traffic to determine when it is safe to cross. Depending on the sounds the user hears, she will command the dog to move forward. If the dog sees a car making a quick turn or veering toward them, the dog must use intelligent disobedience and stay still or, if necessary, back away to protect the handler. The dog's traffic skills are vital

If a guide dog sees a car making a quick turn, it may use intelligent disobedience to move back in order to protect its handler.

For the final phase in traffic training, Guiding Eyes dogs travel to New York City to practice—and prove—their guiding skills.

on modern roads because today's cars, especially electric cars, are quieter and more difficult for a blind person to detect.

For the final phase of traffic training, the pair goes to New York City to practice riding subways and walking on sidewalks filled with people. In this city adventure, the dog gets a chance to prove its guiding skills. After months of targeted training, the guide dog is ready to meet daily challenges with its new user.

Building a Guide Dog Team

Becky Barnes is the Manager of Consumer Outreach and Graduate Support for Guiding Eyes for the Blind. She is also a guide dog user. Barnes has been legally blind since birth, but she has limited vision in one eye. Like many legally blind people, she is able to see some light.

Years ago, Guiding Eyes teamed Barnes with her first guide dog, a female golden retriever named Rowan. After eight years of work, Rowan retired and lived with Barnes and her husband as a pet. Rowan

Becky Barnes depends on Flyer to lead her through her busy days at work and home.

was content to relax in the Barnes's house when the cold New York winds blew, but Barnes still had to venture outside. She needed a working guide dog, so she applied to Guiding Eyes for another canine.

The Guiding Eyes professionals paid a visit the Barnes' home, as they do for all applicants. During a home visit, the experts decide whether or not the person will truly benefit from a guide dog. A guide dog applicant should need a guide dog for more than a jaunt to the mailbox. In order to qualify for a guide dog, Guiding Eyes looks for someone who walks at least four to six blocks daily.

The professionals want to match the right guide dog with the proper handler. They inquire about the person's activity level. For example, does the handler run marathons in his spare time? If yes, he will need a highly energetic dog.

The experts also ask about the person's work requirements. Barnes needed a dog that could commute to the office with her and lie calmly beneath her desk as she worked at the computer. She also required a dog that didn't mind airplanes because she traveled to conferences all around the United States.

The Guiding Eyes experts had a dog in mind for Barnes. Flyer was an adaptable dog that could settle quickly underneath a desk or transit seat.

STUDENT TRAINING

Student training takes place at the Guiding Eyes for the Blind Headquarters and Training Center in Yorktown Heights, New York. The 26-day program teaches students how to work with their future guide dogs.

Before a final decision is made about who will be the dog's future handler, instructors take each student on a Juno walk. During a Juno walk, the instructor holds one end of the harness while the student grasps the handle. The point is to observe the student's walking speed and the length of her stride. Then, the students are teamed with various dogs-in-training in order to see how each student interacts with different dogs. With these activities complete, the instructors make a final decision. For

GUIDING THROUGH DISASTER

On the morning of September 11, 2001, Michael Hingson was working in his office on the 78th floor of the World Trade Center North Tower in New York City. Hingson's guide dog, Roselle, a three-year-old yellow Labrador retriever, was relaxing beneath his desk as her blind user prepared for a presentation.

At 8:46 a.m., Hingson heard a muffled explosion. He felt the building sway. At that moment, terrorists had flown a passenger plane into the building. The airplane crashed 15 floors above Hingson and Roselle.

Hingson's coworker alerted him that flames were shooting from upper story windows, and Hingson realized they needed to escape. He grasped Roselle's harness and verbally directed her to the stairwell. She panted as they descended the hot, crowded stairway. Their noses filled with the stench of jet fuel.

Roselle and Hingson passed firefighters who were on their way up the stairs to save others. They patted Roselle, and she licked their hands. Most of those firefighters would die when the North Tower collapsed. "It was the last act of unconditional love these firefighters got," Hingson has said.

It took 50 minutes for Roselle to guide her handler down all 78 floors and out of the building. They were only 100 yards

Barnes, the trainers were certain that Flyer would be her perfect guide dog.

During training, Barnes and every student learned about caring for their dogs. The guide dog users-in-training were taught to groom and massage their dogs, feed their pups properly, and check the dogs' health. It's important to keep guide

from the area when the South Tower collapsed. Hingson has described the sound from the collapse as a "metal and concrete waterfall." He and Roselle raced through ash and broken glass until they found a subway entrance where they could take shelter.

At one point, they encountered a woman who couldn't see because she had debris in her eyes. Hingson explained that he was a blind man with a guide dog. He took the woman's arm and Roselle guided them both.

Finally, Roselle and Hingson made it to the safety of a friend's home in midtown Manhattan. The teamwork between the dog and user saved both of their lives that day.

Hingson now devotes his days to promoting the wonders of guide dogs. He is the national public affairs representative for Guide Dogs for the Blind in San Raphael, California, where Roselle was raised and trained. Roselle travels the country with Hingson to inspire others and show the importance of teamwork. This hard-working guide dog has won several awards, has met with world leaders, and has appeared on national television shows. Her guiding skills and persistence saved Michael Hingson's life on that fateful day—and have touched countless lives around the world since then.

dogs in top shape so that they can perform their much-needed jobs.

Student training is similar to the formal guide dog training. It begins with basic tasks performed on quiet streets and advances to more complicated maneuvers done in busier areas. The guide dog teams are exposed to all sorts of experiences, such as various traffic situations, train platforms, and grocery stores. The training ends with a trip to Manhattan, where the students and their dogs will test every skill that they learned in the big city.

When the training is complete, a graduation ceremony takes place. Each new guide dog team is recognized for its hard work. The dogs' puppy raisers all earn seats of honor during the celebration. The raisers are awarded a certificate for their care and early training of the pups.

Following graduation, Becky Barnes and Flyer went home to put their skills to use. The time had come for this guide dog team to embark on new journeys together.

A DAY IN THE LIFE

Flyer and Becky Barnes have their schedule down pat. Every morning, Barnes feeds Flyer and then takes him outside for a bathroom break. The pair then commutes to work on a Paratransit bus, a bus designed for disabled people. While Barnes works at her computer, Flyer lies quietly on a pet bed beneath her desk. At lunchtime, the two go for a long walk. After work and dinner, they head out again on another walk and enjoy some playtime together. At night, Flyer sleeps cozily on his own fleece bed in Barnes' room.

Some days, Flyer and Barnes visit schools to teach children about guide dogs. On other days, the pair travels around the country as part of Barnes's job. Flyer helps her board and exit airplanes and wind her way through crowded airports. The team rides in taxis and takes the front seats of buses and trains, which are reserved for the disabled. Flyer is vital to Barnes as she walks along the streets of the cities she visits.

During a recent visit to New York City, Flyer used intelligent disobedience to walk backward from a cab that whipped around a turn. While on another trip, Barnes and three other guide dog users walked to a restaurant for dinner. On the way back to their hotel, the group took a wrong turn. Barnes told Flyer to find the hotel. Above and beyond his guide dog training, Flyer used his keen sense of smell to follow his own scent, which remained from the walk to the restaurant. He brought the group back to the hotel safely.

Service Dogs

A woman in a wheelchair grabs her van keys out of her purse, but they slip through her fingers and fall to the ground. Luckily, she has her service dog to help. The dog retrieves the keys with its mouth and delivers them directly to her hand.

Canine Companions for Independence (CCI) in Santa Rosa, California, breeds and trains service dogs. CCI has its own breeding colony of Labrador and golden retrievers and Lab/golden mixes, called GLXs. These specially-trained canines are taught to perform tasks that might be difficult or painful for a disabled person to attempt. CCI service dogs can benefit a person who suffered a stroke or spinal injury, or someone who has **cerebral palsy** or **multiple sclerosis**.

How does a CCI service dog begin its life in service? Volunteers, known as breeder caregivers, welcome breeding dogs into their homes. The female dog delivers her pups at the home with the help of the breeder caregiver.

When they're two months old, the pups go back to CCI for a series of health checks. Next, young pups are sent to live with puppy raisers in various areas across the United States.

Like many puppy raisers, CCI's volunteers teach dogs basic obedience, like how to sit or stay. In addition to learning to go to the bathroom on the command "hurry," CCI's service dogs are trained to shake paws with people. Plus, the puppies learn to walk loose on a leash rather than pulling on it.

When a puppy is ready to venture out of its neighborhood, the raiser may bring the puppy to the grocery store, the bank, the post office, and other popular spots around town. These visits prepare the puppy to go anywhere that its disabled handler needs to visit.

When the puppy is about 18 months old, it returns to CCI for its "in-for-training" test. This evaluation determines whether or not the dog has what it takes to be a good service dog. For the test, CCI professionals rate the dog's reaction to various situations—much like pups that are "in for training" to be guide dogs.

During the evaluation, a hooded figure pops out from behind a bush and shakes a cane, a heavy metal chain is dragged across a washboard, and a garbage bag is dropped from a tall ladder. Testers watch closely to see how the dog reacts; does it act with confidence and curiosity, or does the dog run and hide? Potential service dogs must take noises in stride because they will come across loud sounds through the day, such as the clanking of a wheelchair lift that helps a disabled person into a van or bus.

FORMAL TRAINING

Dogs that suceed in this first round of testing attend six to nine months of formal service dog training. At first, the trainers teach each canine over 40 service dog commands. For example, the dog learns to "get," or retrieve an item. In addition, the dog is taught to walk backwards when commanded "back."

Service dogs are also taught the command "lap," which prompts the dog to gently place its two front paws on the handler's lap. This command is useful when a disabled person can't reach down to take what the dog has retrieved. The "lap" command brings the dog's mouth close to its user's hands.

Trainers offer the dogs real-life experiences that will help the canines perform service work. The trainers and the dogs pile into a van and visit grocery stores, hospitals, and even busy county fairs. While they are out and about, the dogs learn to be on their best behavior. A service dog is not permitted to chase children or other animals. By teaching service dogs how to behave properly, trainers help prevent dangerous situations. If a service dog bounded away to follow a chipmunk, for example, its handler could be pulled from its wheelchair and injured.

How do service dogs-in-training know if they're doing a good job? CCI's handlers use rewards, such as petting and plenty of praise. If the makes a mistake, its trainer will immediately correct the dog's unwanted behavior with a quick tug and release on the training collar.

Trainers attempt to prepare the dog for life with a disabled handler. The trainers might speak with slower speech or simulate the lack of upper body strength that some disabled individuals have. The trainers realize that some disabled handlers might not be physically able to lean over and hug the dog. For that reason, they train some dogs to be pleased with a scratch on the head from a handler's finger.

JUST LIKE HOME

CCI has two rooms for dogs in training. Light switches line a wall of one of the rooms. There are many types of switches at different heights. The dogs

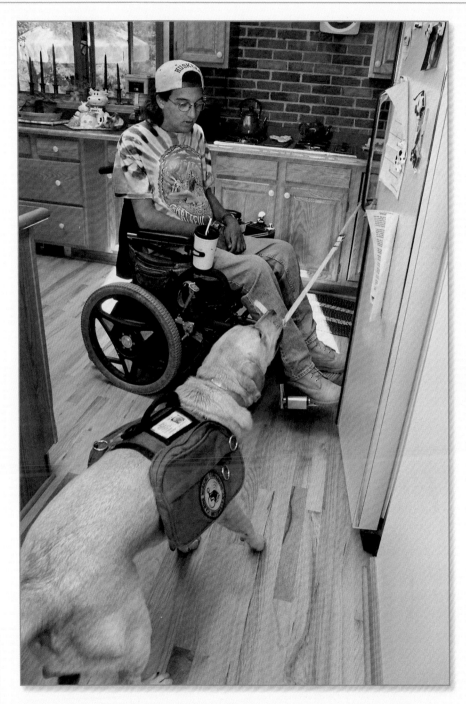

Service dogs may be trained to tug on a strap in order to open cabinets, refrigerators, doors, or drawers.

learn to turn the flip switches on with their noses and off with their paws. If it is a rocker-style switch, the dog uses its nose to work with it.

The training rooms have cabinets and drawers with straps attached to them. The dogs are taught to open each by holding the strap in their mouths and tugging it open. The dogs also learn to push with their noses so that cabinet doors and drawers will close.

CCI provides their dogs with plenty of items so they can practice retrieving. The trainers begin with objects made of materials that are easy for the dogs to hold in their mouths, such as wooden objects. Then,

PSYCHIATRIC SERVICE DOGS

Psychiatric service dogs help people who have been diagnosed with conditions such as depression, panic disorder, or autism.

Depression is a severe and long-lasting feeling of sadness or helplessness. People who have depression might be given medication under a doctor's supervision. Service dogs that work with depression sufferers can be trained to retrieve medicine. These dogs may also be taught to push a certain button on the phone in case of an emergency. That button may be pre-programmed to dial the psychiatrist or mental health crisis hotline.

Psychiatric service dogs may also work with people who suffer bouts of extreme fear, known as **panic attacks**. During a panic attack, a person's heart may race, or he may feel shortness of breath or dizziness. These dogs are trained to brace themselves the dogs learn to pick up items made of metal or plastic. By the time the dogs complete training, they will be able to retrieve a thin credit card and deliver it across the counter to a store clerk. These skills help disabled users to cope with in daily life situations.

MAKING A MATCH

People who want to use service dogs from CCI attend a two-week school to learn to work with their dogs. Before matching a dog to its handler, trainers consider the student's personality and daily life activities. A college student who plays wheelchair basketball

and stand stiff so that their users can lean on them until the panic attack passes.

Cindy Vandawalker is the head trainer for Canine Working Companions in Waterville, New York. She trained a yellow Labrador retriever, named Cleo, for a 12-year-old girl with **autism**. Someone with autism might behave as though she lives in a world of her own. She might have trouble communicating with others. Sometimes, autistic people repeat certain actions, such as arm flapping or head-banging.

Because of her autism, the girl was uncomfortable leaving home, but that changed when Cleo stepped into her life. "Cleo opened a new door for her," Vandawalker reports.

The two go for walks together and visit the mall. If the girl feels overwhelmed, she hugs and pets her dog until she feels calm. Cleo and other psychiatric service dogs give people a chance to live more fulfilling and independent lives.

in her spare time, for example, might need a dog with boundless energy. Yet, a person who works at a computer all day might require a relaxed, patient dog. Trainers want to make sure that both the handler and the dog are satisfied with one another.

After graduation, handlers and their dogs often work together for additional training. Each user can expand on the dog's commands and training to fit her particular lifestyle needs. A person might use the "tug" command to have the dog pull clothes from

People can train service dogs to help with specific tasks, such as using the "tug" command to pull off socks.

the drier, for instance, or to remove his socks when he undresses. If its handler is thirsty, for example, the dog can tug open the refrigerator door, retrieve a bottle of water with its mouth, close the door with its nose, and deliver the cold water to its handler. The possibilities for training a service dog are endless.

7 Hearing Dogs

Picture this: A family brings a homemade cake to the home of their new neighbor. The family knocks several times and waits. When there's no answer, the family heads back to their home, disappointed. They don't know that their new neighbor is deaf and couldn't hear the knock.

Now, consider this scenario. The neighbors knock, and on the other side of the door, a dog perks up its ears and runs to the door to check for the source of the sound. The dog races back to its handler, nudges her with its nose, and leads her to the door. The neighbors greet each other and share a slice of cake.

In addition to training service dogs, Canine Companions for Independence (CCI) trains dogs to help deaf people and those who have trouble hearing. After CCI's dogs pass their in-for-training test, they go to a trainer for up to two months. While the trainers work with the dogs, they pay close attention to the canine's personality. If a dog is extremely attentive to what is happening, has extra energy, and really loves food, the dog may be recommended to enter training as a hearing dog.

The first step is to test to see if the dogs would make effective hearing dogs. To do this, a trainer places a dog in a room and sets off a variety of sounds, such as a ringing telephone or a beeping smoke alarm. The trainer wants to find a dog that pays attention to the sound and investigates it.

At one point in the test, a trainer places a piece of dog kibble under her palm. The trainers look for a dog that is persistent in pursuit of the food. Perhaps the dog will nudge the trainer's hand with its nose or paw. Sometimes, the dog will perform a trick that has resulted in a treat in the past. The trainers need the hearing dog to be determined and, at times, a bit pushy about reaching a goal. This skill comes in handy in situations when a deaf user is asleep and

THERAPY DOGS

Someone who has had a stroke may suffer from a weakened arm. A therapy dog that has been trained to help people regain their health may work with a stroke patient to help her recover her strength. As the patient uses her arm to throw a ball for a game of fetch, her arm becomes stronger and stronger.

Canine Working Companions in Waterville, New York, trains therapy dogs. These dogs are usually owned by ordinary people who have attended weeks of training to teach their dogs skills that could be useful for hospital patients. Therapy dogs can be nearly any breed imaginable, from border collies to German shepherds. During training, dogs learn to obey their handlers and act calmly in all situations. The dogs are exposed to the types of noises they might hear in a hospital or **rehabilitation** facility. They are taught

(continues)

Some therapy dogs are trained to paw a book and listen patiently in order to help students improve their reading skills.

(continued)

to stay calm despite the rattle of a walker, or the clanking of metal trays, or the beeps of a machine.

Some therapy dogs are trained to visit libraries and schools. Their job is to aid children who are having trouble reading. How can a therapy dog help teach reading? The dog could lie on a blanket and listen while a child reads a book aloud. The dog places its paw on the page as it has been trained to do. Children who have trouble reading often feel at ease when reading to a dog because no one is judging them or laughing at them as they read. Reading to and petting a friendly dog certainly doesn't seem like schoolwork, which makes reading that much more fun!

cannot hear an alarm clock buzzing or a fire alarm blaring. A hearing dog must keep nudging until its handler is awake.

SOUND TRAINING

If a dog succeeds at the temperament test, formal hearing dog training begins. Teaching the proper hearing dog behavior is complex work, so the CCI training is broken into smaller steps. At first, the dog is taught to nudge the trainer two or three times with its nose. Next, three kitchen timers are placed in different kennels. One timer is activated, and the dog learns to find the buzzing timer. When it correctly locates the object, the dog is rewarded with food. The difficulty of this task is increased by including more timers and by placing the activated timer farther away. Eventually, sounds, such as doorbells and alarm clocks, are added.

During these lessons, trainers pet or play with the dogs to distract them from investigating the sound. However, a hearing dog in training must not allow anything to interfere with its search. Keeping the attention on the sound is of utmost importance.

"Hearing dogs learn that sound overrides anything," says Amy McPherson, a CCI instructor. "The dogs learn that even if they have a down-stay command, sound overrides it." In this way, a hearing dog uses intelligence to disobey a command. The dog must find the sound despite the handler's command.

Finally, the dogs are taught to lead the trainers to the sound when they ask, "What?" Because some people who are deaf cannot speak, hearing dogs are taught to respond to spoken words and modified American Sign Language signs. The modified signs only require one hand to form a command.

After learning how to consistently alert the trainers to sounds, canines are ready to advance to the training apartment. The training apartment is a room designed to look similar to the inside of a house. The room even has a bathroom and patio to **simulate** a real home.

In the apartment, the trainers take their places. One trainer plays the part of the deaf handler, completing everyday tasks around the training apartment. She might wash dishes, brush her teeth, or watch television. Another trainer stays in the control room, where she activates a variety of sounds in the apartment. This person can see directly into the training room through a one-way mirror.

During the apartment training, the dog might be called upon to alert the trainer and take her to the oven timer or the telephone. When it comes to the sound of a smoke alarm, though, the dog is taught to alert in a very specialized way. Instead of bringing the trainer to the source of the noisy alarm, the dog leads the trainer to an exit door. This behavior will keep the dog's future handler from encountering a fire.

LEARNING TO HANDLE

CCI's prospective hearing dog handlers attend a two-week training course to learn to work with their dogs. When the handlers return home with their canine companions, they might **customize** their dog's skills to suit their individual needs. A handler might teach the dog to alert her to a baby's cry or to the sound of a doorbell ringing. The dog could learn to let his handler know when the tea kettle whistles or the cell phone rings, for example. Dogs that accompany their owners to work or in the car

Hearing dogs are important because they keep their deaf or hearing-impaired handlers aware of the sounds around them.

can be trained to alert their owners to car horns or emergency vehicle sirens.

Hearing dogs keep their handlers aware of important sounds around them. These dogs and other helping dogs like them play a very important role in the lives of human beings. They work hard to make sure their handlers are safe and secure. Along the way, the dogs get plenty of praise, encouragement, and love for what they do best: help people.

Glossary

Autism brain disorder that causes affected individuals to have problems with social interaction and communication

Cerebral palsy a disorder caused by damage to the brain before, during, or after birth. It can cause loss of muscle coordination and speech difficulties

Customize made or done to suit a personal taste or need

Depression a severe and long-time feeling of sadness or helplessness

Intelligent disobedience a dog's ability, developed through extensive training, to ignore a command in order to keep its handler safe

Multiple sclerosis a disease characterized by a loss of myelin and the formation of scar tissue near the nerves, which may result in paralysis

Panic attack sudden severe anxiety accompanied by shortness of breath, rapid heartbeat, or dizziness

Rehabilitation the act of restoring to health

Simulate to create a model of

Socializers people who introduce the puppies to social situations, such as interacting with others and visiting different places

Temperament mental or emotional traits

Bibliography

Angstrom, Melinda (Guiding Eyes for the Blind, Class Supervisor). Interview with the author. Yorktown Heights, N.Y. May 19, 2005.

Barnes, Becky (Guiding Eyes for the Blind, Manager of Consumer Outreach and guide dog user). Telephone interview with the author. June 15, 2005.

Blake, Bill (Canine Companions for Independence, National Public Relations Manager). Telephone interview with the author. July 19, 2005.

Clough, Christina (Guiding Eyes for the Blind, Senior Whelping Technician). Interview with the author. Patterson, N.Y. August 3, 2004.

Curry, Woody. (Guiding Eyes for the Blind, Apprentice Instructor). Interview with the author. Yorktown Heights, N.Y. February 23, 2005.

Davis, Kathy Diamond. *Therapy Dogs: Training Your Dog to Reach Others*. Wenatchee, WA: Dogwise, 2002.

Frank Morris. *First Lady of the Seeing Eye*. New York: Pyramid Books, 1957.

Froling, Joan. "Assistance Dog Tasks." International Association of Assistance Dog Partners. www.iaadp.org/tasks.html

Froling, Joan. "Service Dog Tasks for Psychiatric Disabilities." June 20, 2003, International Association of Assistance Dog Partners. www.iaadp.org/psd_tasks.html

Fulk, Libby (Guiding Eyes for the Blind, Puppy Evaluator). Interview with the author. Patterson, N.Y. January 28, 2005.

Hingson, Michael. "The Path to Safety: A survivor of the World Trade Center tragedy tells his story." *Guide Dog News*. Fall 2001. http://www.guidedogs.com/news-Hingson.html

Iwanicki, Vikki (Guiding Eyes for the Blind Canine Development Center, Program Manager). Interviews with the author. Patterson, New York. August 3, 2004 and January 28, 2005. Yorktown Heights, N.Y. February 19, 2005.

Juckett, William (Guiding Eyes for the Blind guide dog user). Telephone interview with the author. October 16, 2004.

Martine, Andrea (Guiding Eyes for the Blind, Special Needs Trainer). Interview with the author. Yorktown Heights, N.Y. February 23, 2005.

McPherson, Amy (Canine Companions for Independence, Instructor). Telephone interview with the author. July 28, 2005.

Montero, David. "Guide Dog Led Owner Downstairs on 9/11: Man tells story to persuade people to raise guide puppies." *Ventura County Star.* April 25, 2003.

Nordin, Lee (Guiding Eyes for the Blind, Director of Canine Development). Interview with the author. Patterson, N.Y. January 28, 2005.

Purcell, Ellin (Guiding Eyes for the Blind, Director of Special Needs Program). Interviews with the author. Yorktown Heights, N.Y. February 2, 2005 and May 19, 2005.

Ravetto, Christine, Mark, and Nicole (Guiding Eyes for the Blind, puppy raisers). Interview with the author. Patterson, N.Y. August 3, 2004.

Russenburger, Jane (Guiding Eyes for the Blind, Senior Director of Breeding and Placement). E-mail discussion with the author. February 25, 2005.

Stoga, Gloria Gilbert (Puppies Behind Bars, President). Telephone interview with the author. June 9, 2005.

Vandawalker, Cindy (Canine Working Companions, Head Trainer). Telephone interview with the author. August 7, 2005.

Williams, Chris. *Lady.* Warwick, N.Y.: Moo Press, 2004.

Williams, Clover (Guiding Eyes for the Blind, Reproduction and Cryogenics Manager). Interview with the author. Patterson, N.Y. August 3, 2004.

Zubrycki, Kathy (Guiding Eyes for the Blind, Director of Training and Admissions). Interview with the author. Yorktown Heights, N.Y. February 2, 2005.

For More Information

Find out more about the training and work of the dogs in this book by contacting these organizations.

Canine Companions for Independence
P.O. Box 446
Santa Rosa, California 95402-0446
1-866-224-3647
www.caninecompanions.org

Canine Working Companions
P.O. Box 2128
Syracuse, New York 13220-2128
1-315-656-3301
www.canineworkingcompanions.org

The Delta Society
875 124th Ave. NE Suite 101
Bellevue, Washington 98005
1-425-226-7357
www.deltasociety.org

Guide Dogs for the Blind
P.O. Box 151200
San Rafael, California 94915-1200
1-800-295-4050
www.guidedogs.com

Guiding Eyes for the Blind Canine Development Center
361 Route 164
Patterson, New York 12563
1-845-878-3330
www.cdc.guidingeyes.org

Guiding Eyes for the Blind Headquarters and Training Center
611 Granite Springs Road
Yorktown Heights, New York 10598
1-914-245-4024
www.guidingeyes.org

Puppies Behind Bars
10 E. 40th Street 19th Floor
New York, New York 10016
1-212-680-9562
www.puppiesbehindbars.org

The Seeing Eye
P.O. Box 375
Morristown, New Jersey 07963-0375
1-973-539-4425
www.seeingeye.org

Further Reading

Dibsie, Patricia. *Love Heels: Tales from Canine Companions for Independence.* New York: Yorkville Press, 2003.

Gorrell, Gena K. *Working Like a Dog.* Toronto, Ontario: Tundra, 2003.

Kent, Deborah. *Animal Helpers for the Disabled.* New York: Franklin Watts, 2003.

Lawrenson, Diana. *Guide Dogs: From Puppies to Partners.* Australia: Allen & Unwin Pty. Ltd., 2002

McDaniel, Melissa. *Guide Dogs.* New York: Bearport Publishing Company, Inc., 2005.

Moore, Eva. *Buddy: The First Seeing Eye Dog.* New York: Scholastic, Inc., 1996.

Patent, Dorothy Hinshaw. *The Right Dog for the Job: Ira's Path from Service Dog to Guide Dog.* New York: Walker & Company, 2004.

Presnall, Judith Janda. *Hearing Dogs.* San Diego: Kidhaven Press, 2004.

Tagliaferro, Linda. *Therapy Dogs.* New York: Bearport Publishing Company, Inc., 2005.

Web Sites

Assistance Dogs International Inc.
www.adionline.org
Read about how various assistance dogs are trained.

Dogs for the Deaf, Inc.
www.dogsforthedeaf.org
Learn how this group adopts dogs from shelters and trains them
to help people.

Fidelco Guide Dog Foundation
www.fidelco.org
Learn why German shepherds make good guide dogs.

Guide Dogs of America
www.guidedogsofamerica.org
Read about the group's mission to provide free guide dogs to
people in the U.S. and Canada.

National Service Dogs
www.nsd.on.ca
Check out how children with autism and special needs benefit
from service dogs.

Therapy Dogs International, Inc.
www.tdi-dog.org
See how dogs helped Hurricane Katrina victims cope.

The Bright and Beautiful Therapy Dogs, Inc.
www.golden-dogs.org
Explore how your dog can become a certified therapy dog.

Picture Credits

Index